The life and times of Shelly & Sheldon

By: Bryan Heydon

I dedicate this picture book to my two loving pet Russian Tortoises.

(Shelly & Sheldon)

Obviously The two models for this book.

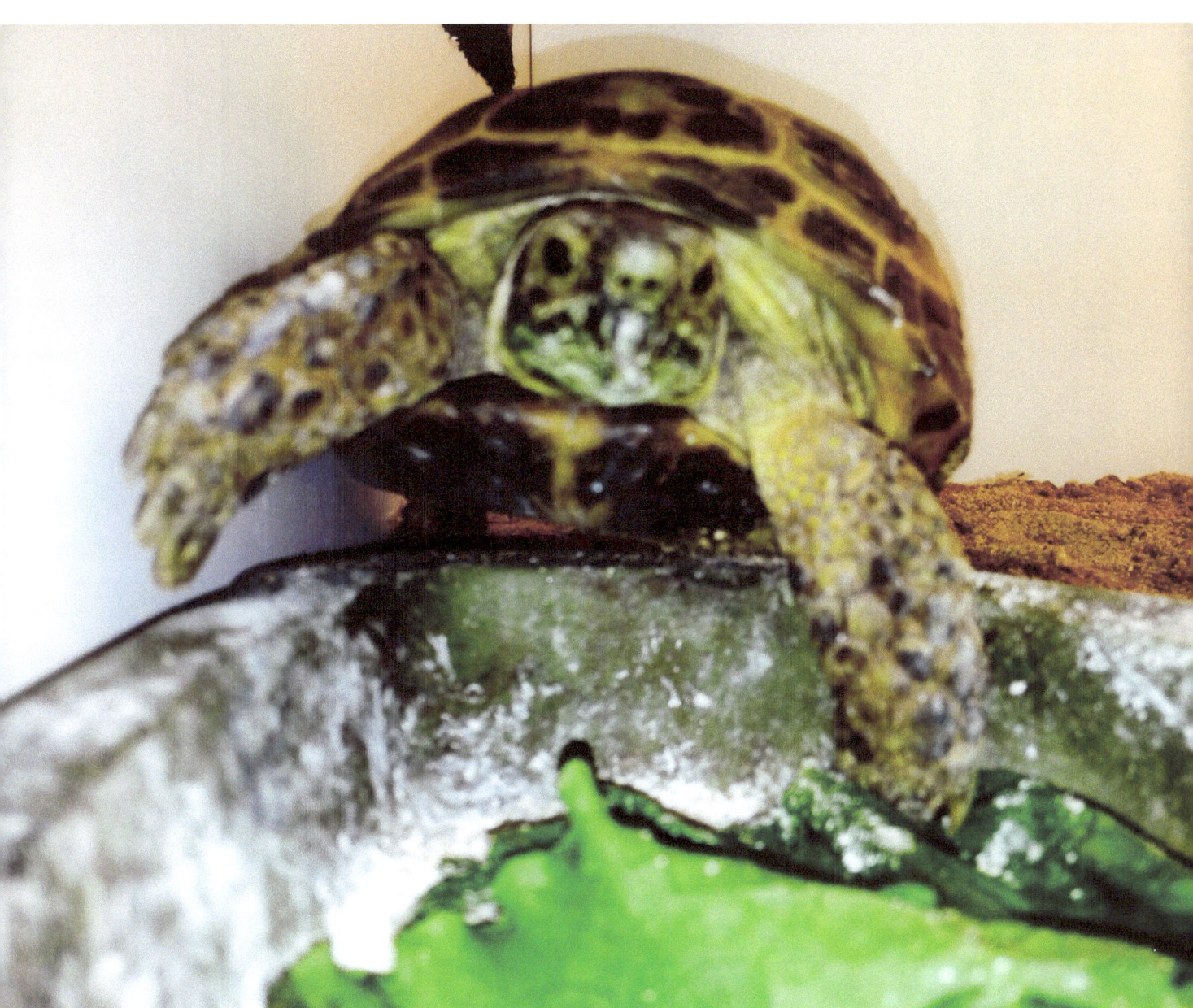

Here we have Sheldon coming in for a closer look at the camera.

Don't worry the white stuff he is playing in is left over calcium powder from his meal lol.

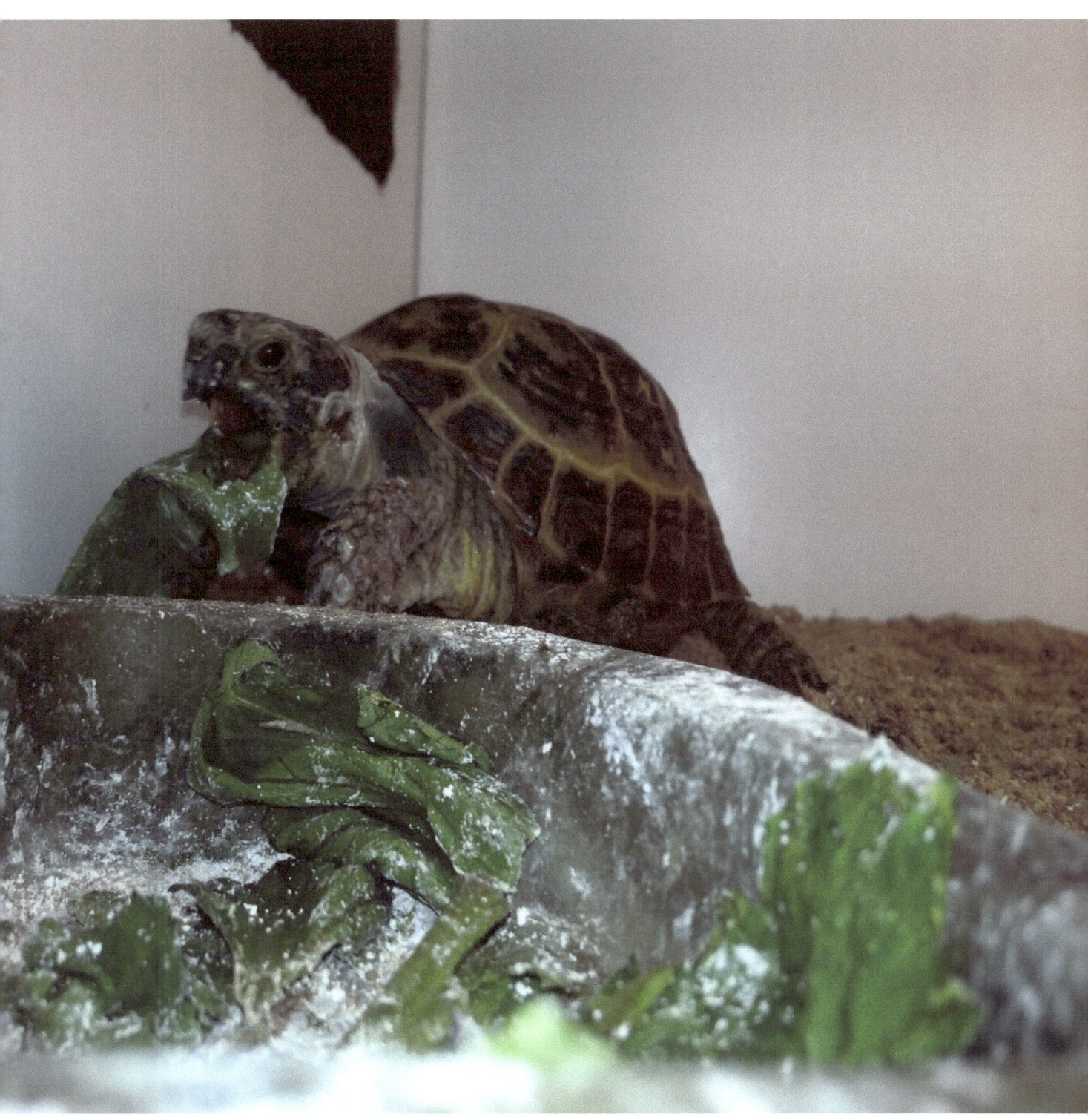

Here's Sheldon again chomping away at his lettuce with calcium powder

Lol!

Very cute.

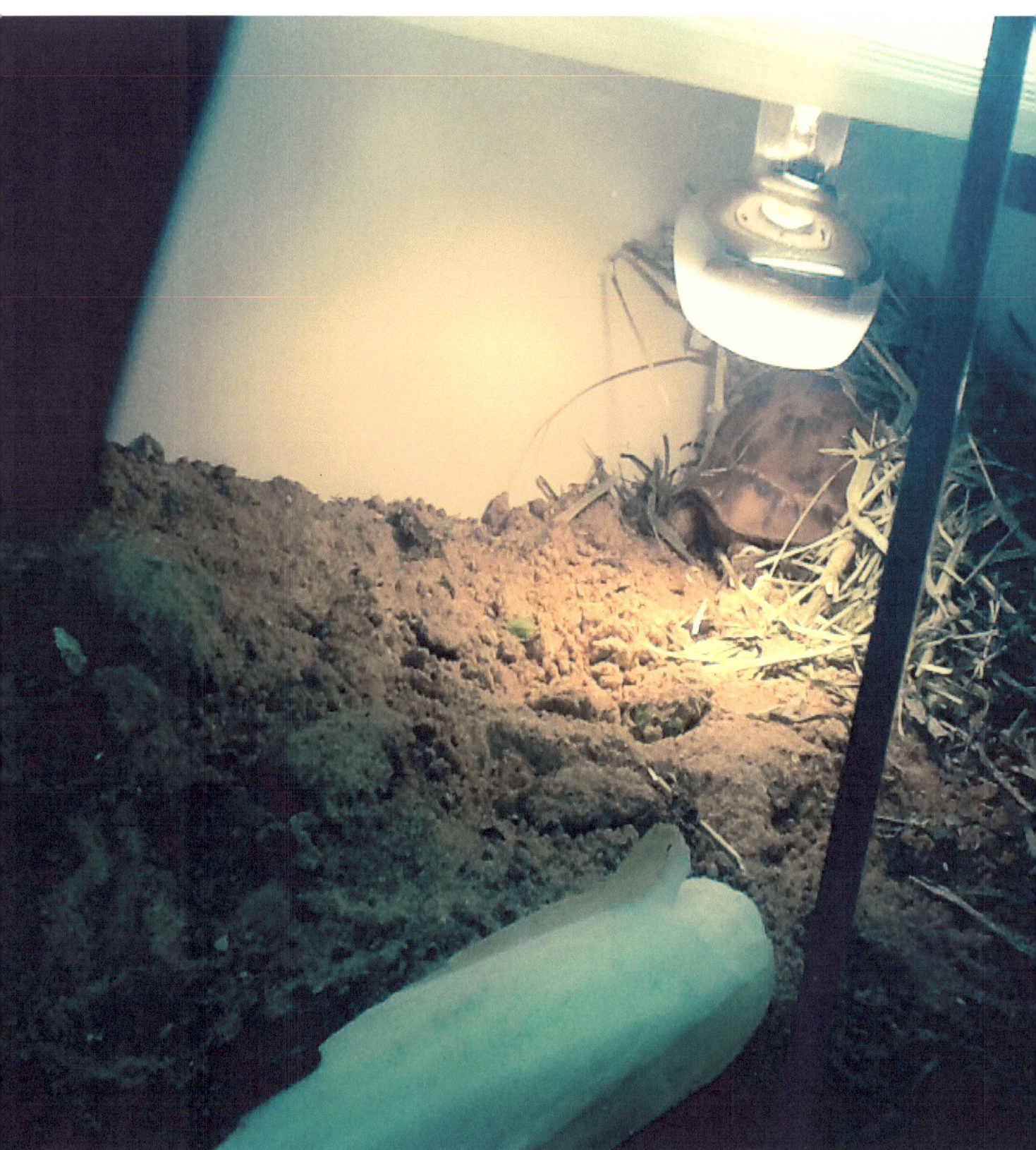

Here we have shelly being a lazy bum.

She has a little corner to be snug in.

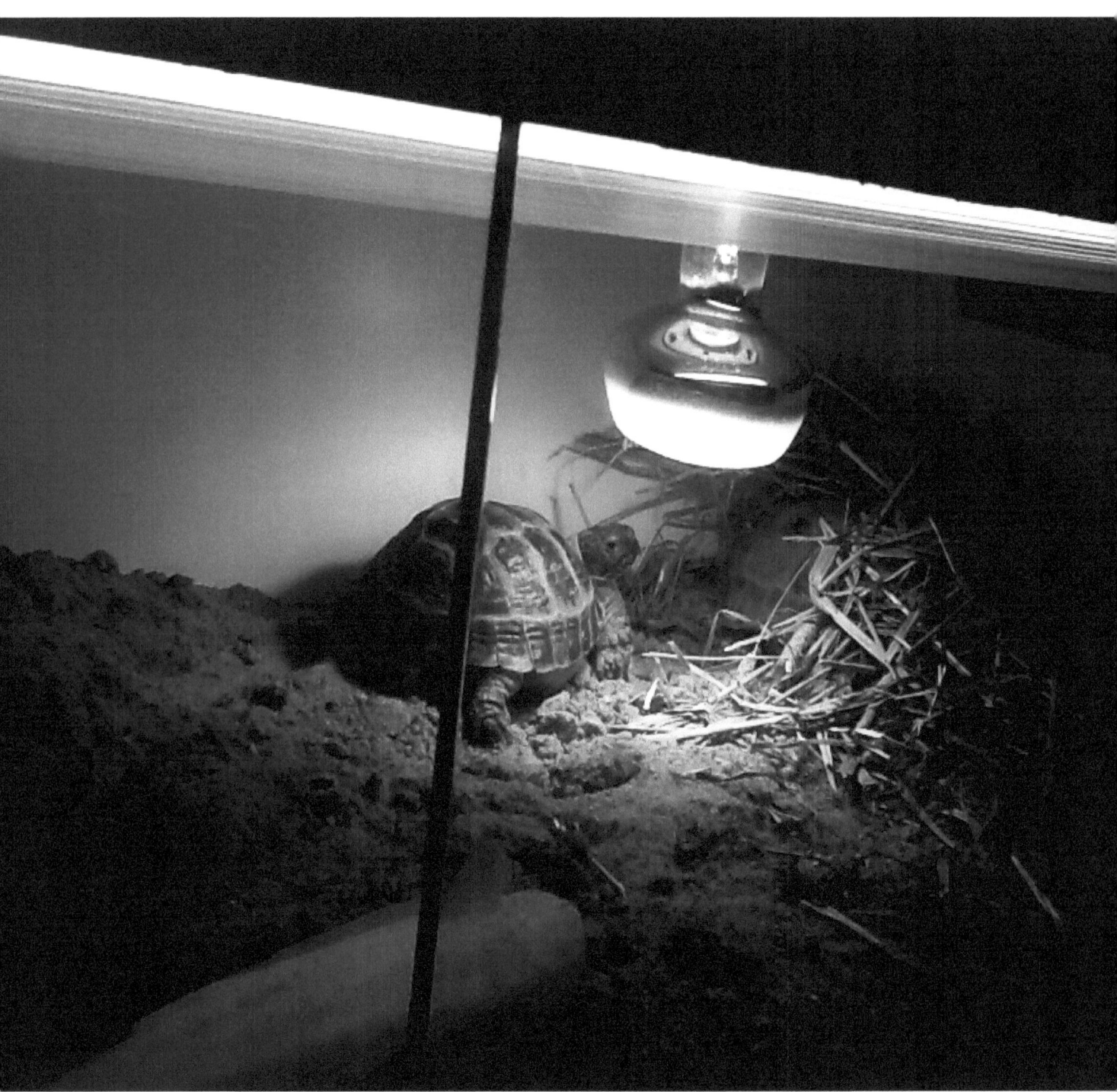

UH OH!

Here comes Sheldon to check
out what shelly is up too!

On to the next caption

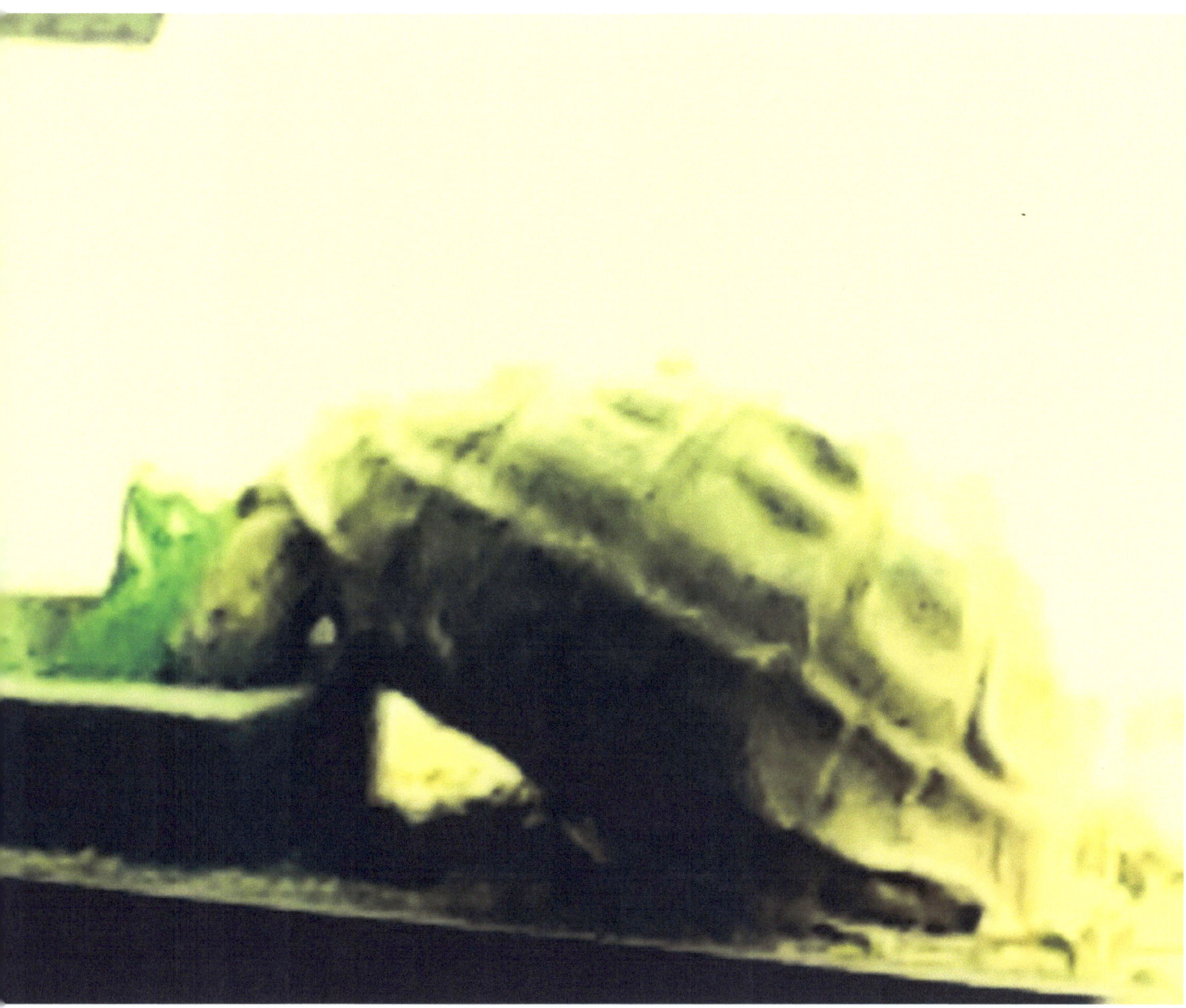

Look at that! Now Shelly is eating. Good for her. Eat up Shelly.

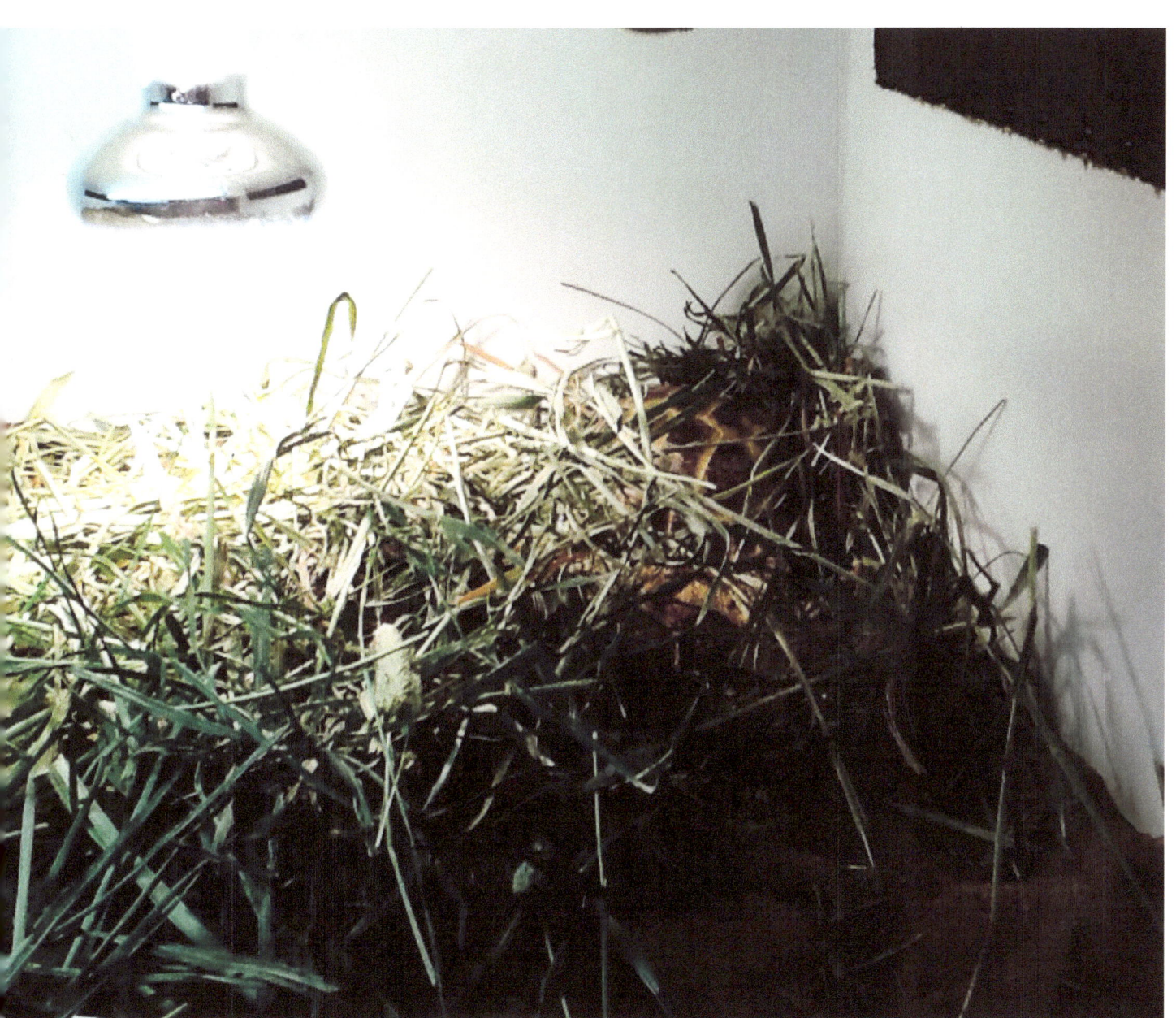

AWWW! Look at that!

Sheldon is sleeping.

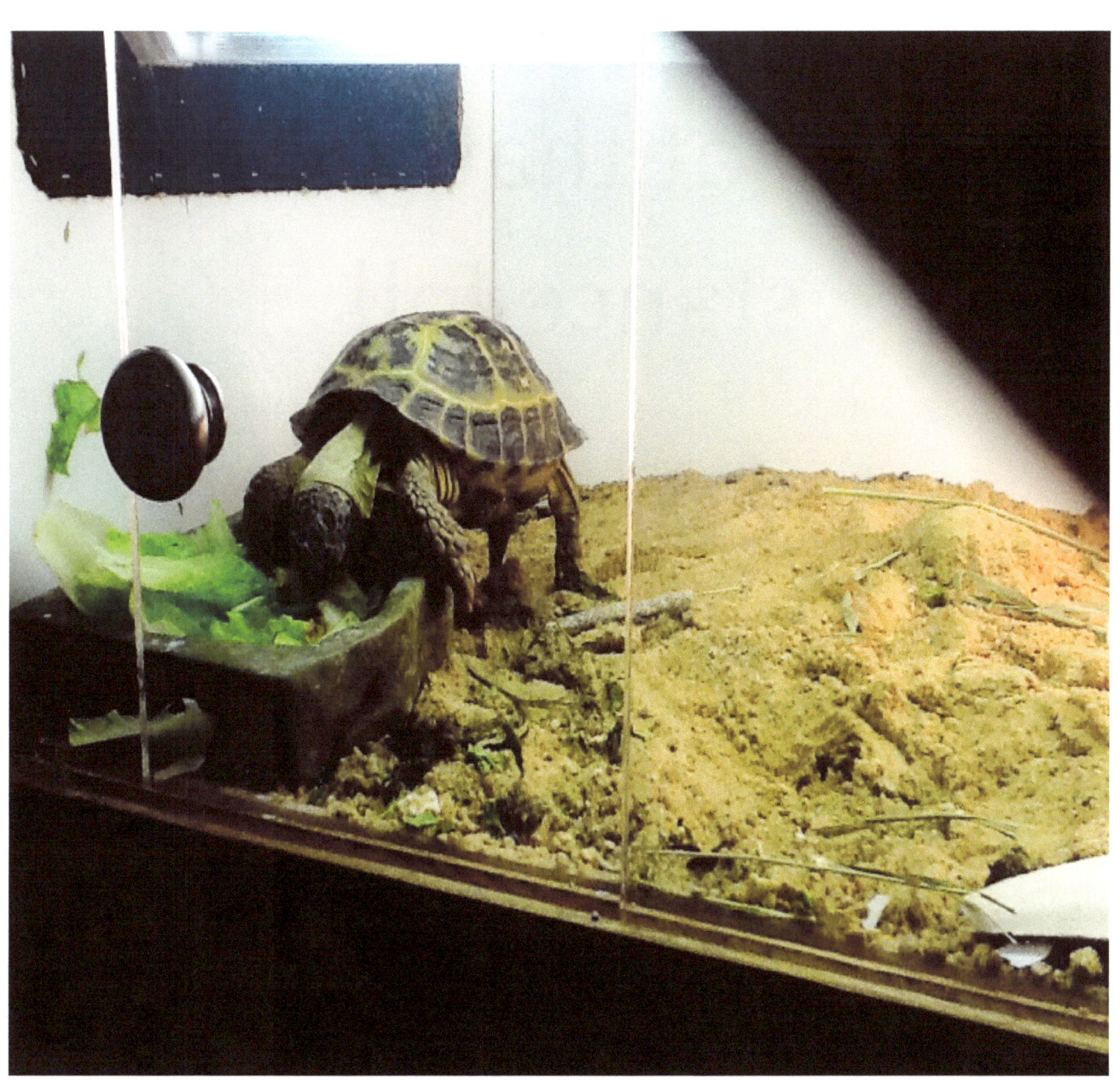

Look at that goofy stance lol!

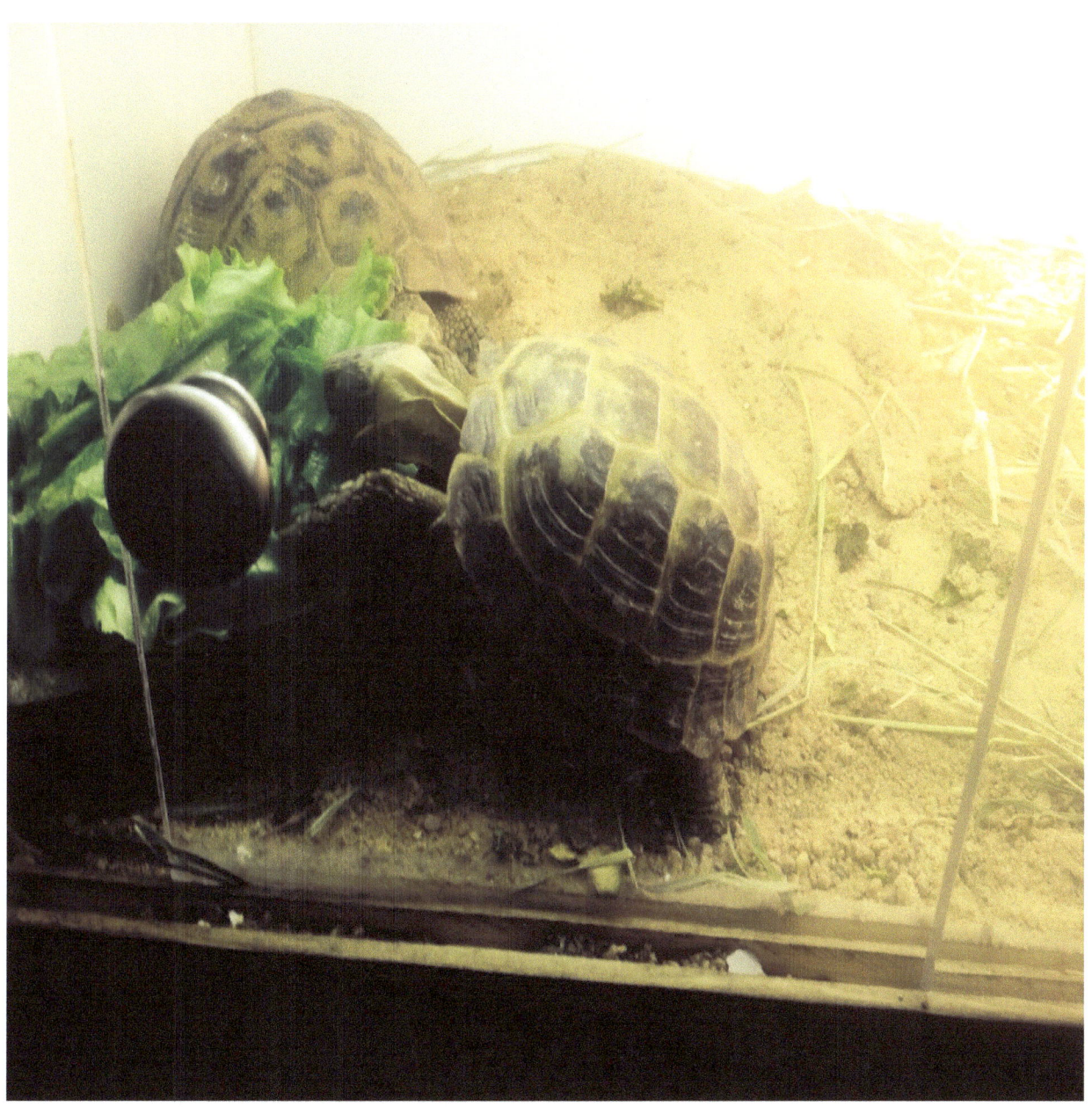

They are starting to eat together how friendly.

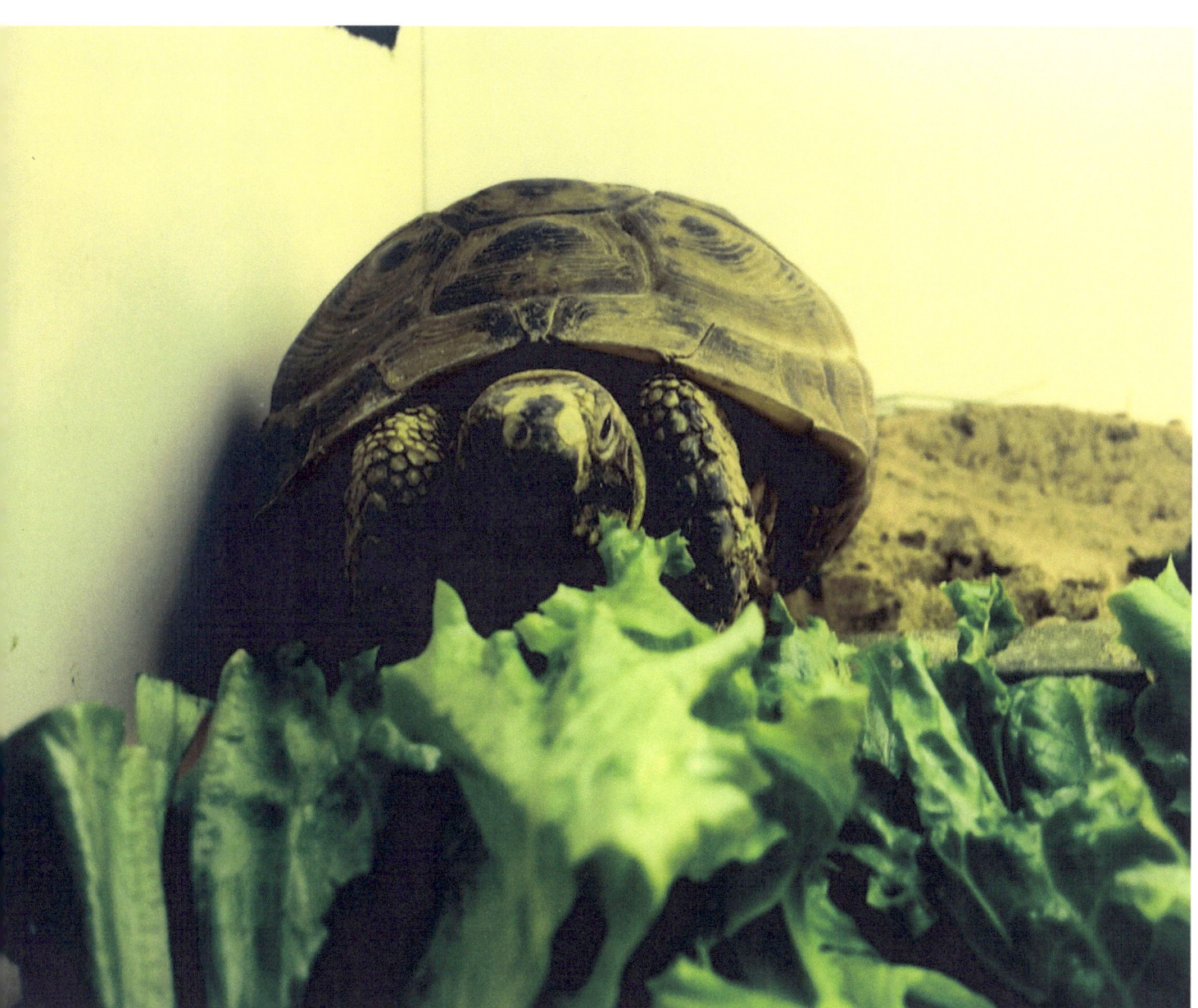

Face to face with shelly!

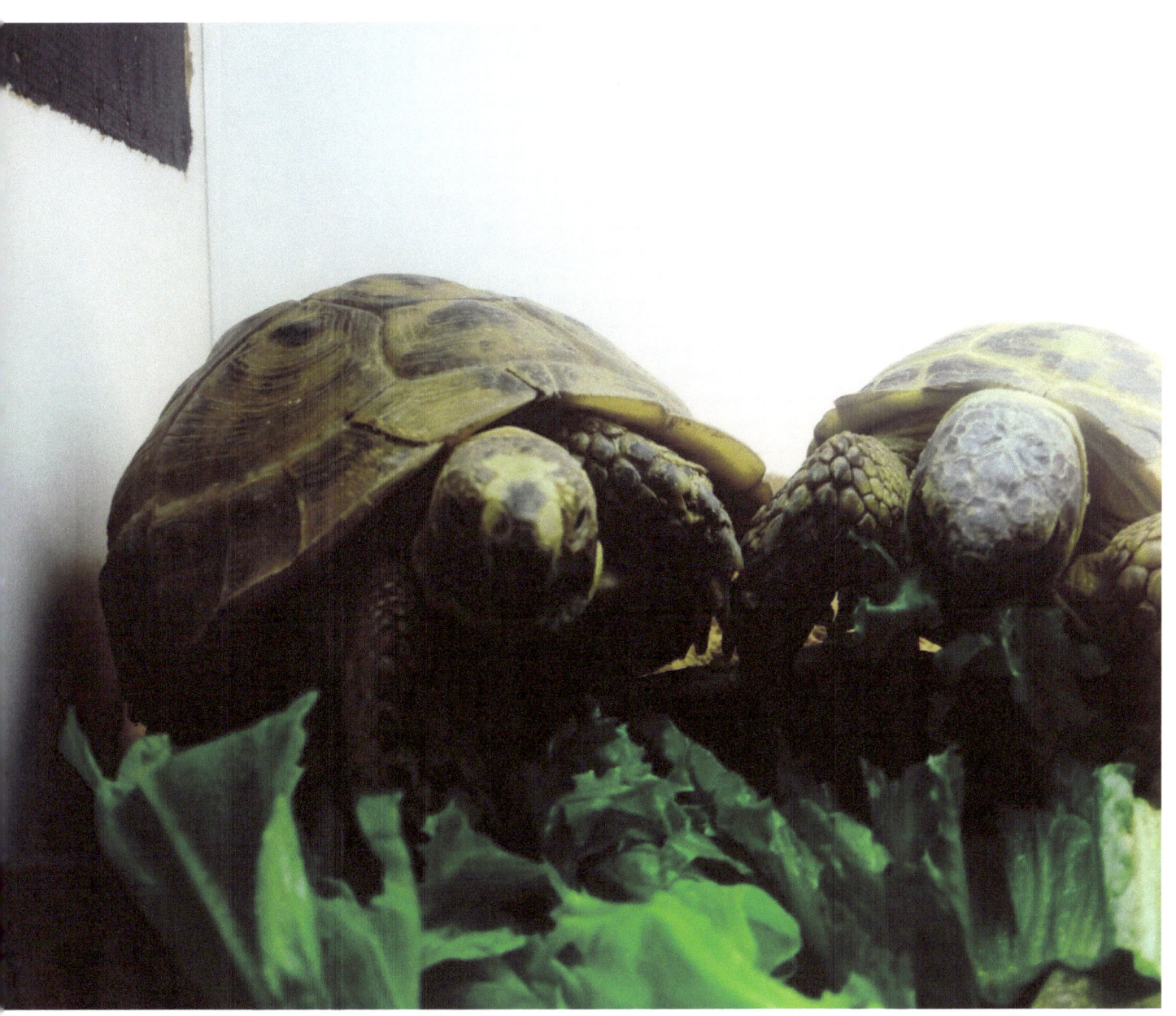

AAAwwww! It's like they're holding hands while they eat!

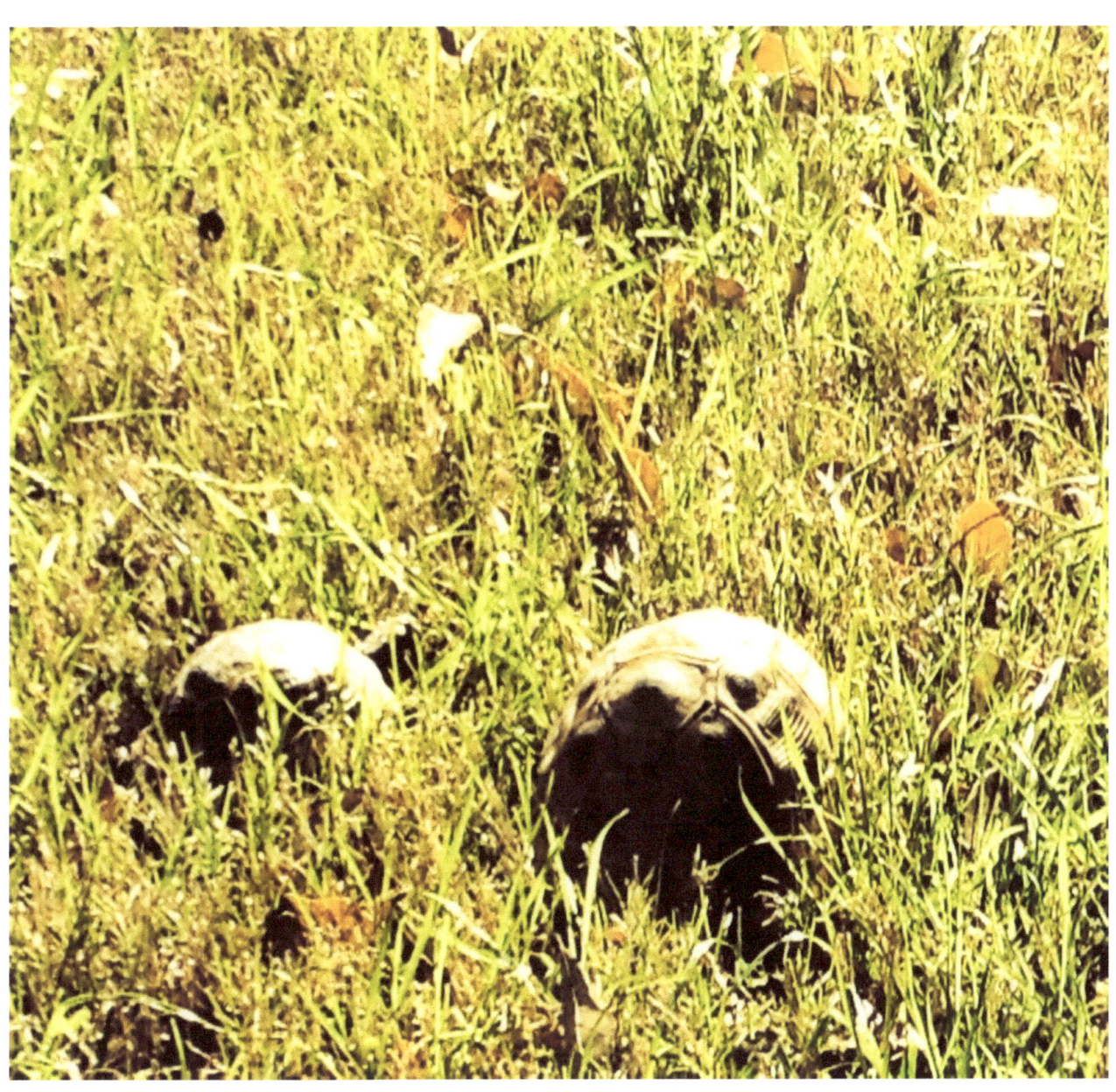

Outside together!

The End